Meet the Ring-Tailed Lemur

Suzanne Buckingham

PowerKiDS press

New York

For the Prondzinski family—Mark, Lisa, and Lukas

Published in 2009 by The Rosen Publishing Group, Inc.
29 East 21st Street, New York, NY 10010

First Edition

Editor: Joanne Randolph
Book Design: Greg Tucker
Photo Researcher: Jessica Gerweck

Photo Credits: Cover, cover (logo), back cover, pp. 5, 10, 12–13, 15, 16, 19, 20 Shutterstock.com; p. 6 © National Geographic/Getty Images; p. 9 © Kevin Schafer/Getty Images.

Library of Congress Cataloging-in-Publication Data

Buckingham, Suzanne.
  Meet the ring-tailed lemur / Suzanne Buckingham. — 1st ed.
      p. cm. — (Scales and tails)
  Includes index.
  ISBN 978-1-4042-4501-3 (library binding)
  1. Ring-tailed lemur—Juvenile literature. I. Title.
  QL737.P95B83 2009
  599.8'3—dc22
                                        2008007744

Manufactured in the United States of America

CPSIA Compliance Information: Batch# CR105010PK: For further information contact Rosen Publishing, New York, New York at 1-800-237-9932.

Contents

Meet the Ring-Tailed Lemur

Maybe you have seen a ring-tailed lemur at the zoo. Did you notice its long, striped tail and its big eyes? Lemurs are furry **mammals** that like to climb trees. There are about 40 kinds of lemurs in the world. The ring-tailed lemur has a white face, with a dark mask around its eyes. It weighs between 5 and 7 ½ pounds (2–3 kg) and is about the size of a cat.

The ring-tailed lemur is famous for its long, black-and-white-striped tail. This tail measures about 2 feet (61 cm) and is longer than its body.

When a ring-tailed lemur walks, its tail stands up and curls at the tip.

This ring-tailed lemur makes its way along the forest floor on all four feet. Ring-tailed lemurs can also hop on their two back feet.

Island Living

Ring-tailed lemurs and all other wild lemurs live on an island near the southeast coast of Africa called Madagascar. Madagascar is the fourth-largest island in the world. It is surrounded by the Indian Ocean. Ring-tailed lemurs are generally found on the south end of this warm, sunny island.

The ring-tailed lemurs living on Madagascar are considered **endangered** animals. The number of ring-tailed lemurs in the wild has dropped because the forests where they make their homes are disappearing. People have cleared the land to grow coffee and other crops.

At Home in the Trees

Ring-tailed lemurs make their homes in different kinds of forests. Some live in thick, green rain forests, where beautiful flowers and trees filled with colorful fruit grow. Ring-tailed lemurs also live in dry forests filled with cacti and trees with sharp **spines**.

Ring-tailed lemurs are **arboreal** animals. This means they spend most of their time in trees. As they jump from tree to tree, ring-tailed lemurs use their tails for balance. They also walk across the forest floor. At night, these furry animals lay on large tree branches to sleep.

A ring-tailed lemur sits on the pointy branches of a tree in one of Madagascar's spiny forests.

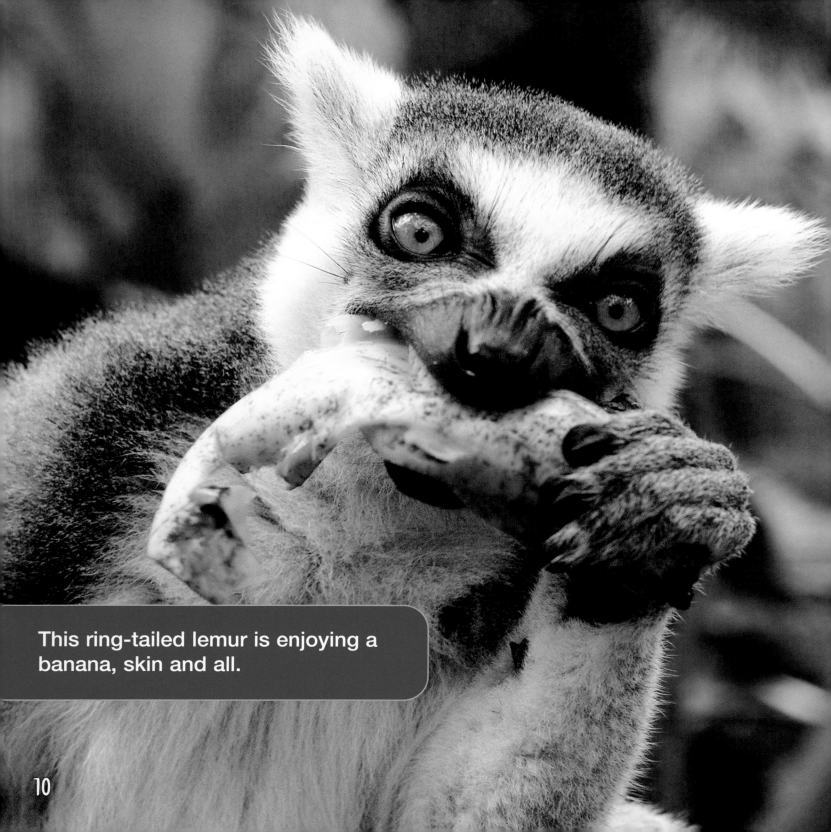

This ring-tailed lemur is enjoying a banana, skin and all.

Lunching Lemurs

Most ring-tailed lemurs are herbivores. This means they eat only plants. They like sweet, juicy fruit best. Ring-tailed lemurs also enjoy leaves and tasty flowers. They eat tree **bark** and sticky sap, too.

Some hungry lemurs dine on spiders, grasshoppers, and other bugs. These ring-tailed lemurs are called omnivores because they eat both plants and animals.

Ring-tailed lemurs that live in dry forests must search for a drink of water when they get thirsty. Sometimes, lemurs drink the dewdrops found on plants in the morning. Lemurs also drink juice from the thick leaves of certain cactus plants.

The Ring-Tailed Lemur

The hands, feet, and ears of a ring-tailed lemur are white. Its face is mostly white, too, with the eyes and nose ringed in black.

Tail Tales

- Ring-tailed lemurs usually walk on all four paws, but sometimes they will walk on their two back paws for a short time.
- A ring-tailed lemur's back legs are longer than its front ones.
- Ring-tailed lemurs like to sunbathe every morning. They sit facing the Sun and warm themselves after a cold night.
- The striped tail of a ring-tailed lemur has about 13 black and 13 white bands.
- Ring-tailed lemurs in the wild live to be about 16 years old.
- The word lemur means "ghost" in the language spoken on Madagascar.
- Ring-tailed lemurs have up to 15 kinds of calls. Each call sends a different message to other lemurs.
- Just like you, ring-tailed lemurs sleep at night and are awake during the day.

Group Living

The ring-tailed lemur is a **social** animal. It likes to be with other lemurs. A group of lemurs is called a troop. One troop usually has between 6 and 30 animals in it. Members of a troop often sunbathe, eat, and sleep together.

A troop has both males and females, but its leader is a female. Female ring-tailed lemurs are strong. They always win in fights against males.

When it is time to **mate**, male ring-tailed lemurs often leave their troops. Males search for females to mate with in other troops.

Here a troop of lemurs spends time together on the ground. Troops can travel up to 3 ½ miles (6 km) each day to find food.

Ring-tailed lemurs talk to each other by making sounds and faces. What do you think this lemur is trying to say?

All Talk?

Ring-tailed lemurs have many ways to **communicate** with each other. The way a lemur holds its body or the look on its face often sends important messages to other lemurs. They also use their voices to make many different calls. For example, a lemur will meow, like a cat, to keep its troop together.

Lemurs use smell to communicate, too. They have **scent glands** on their arms and chests. Ring-tailed lemurs mark paths where they find good food with their scent. Male lemurs keep unwanted lemurs away by rubbing their tails on scent glands and then shaking their smelly tails.

It's a Lemur Life

A little over four months after mating, female ring-tailed lemurs give birth to baby lemurs. New lemurs, called infants, are born in August or September. Mother lemurs usually have one baby, but sometimes they have twins.

Newborns drink milk from their mothers. Infants are **weaned** after about four to six months. Baby lemurs hold themselves close to their mothers' bellies for the first two weeks. Later, infants catch rides on their mothers' backs.

Lemurs reach their adult size when they are one and a half years old. Females can have babies of their own when they are two.

Here a mother ring-tailed lemur holds her babies. When she walks, the babies will take a ride on her back.

These ring-tailed lemurs are grooming each other. They use their tongues and their tooth combs.

Keeping Clean

Ring-tailed lemurs like to **groom** themselves and other lemurs. They use their teeth, instead of fingers, for this cleaning job. Ring-tailed lemurs have six lower teeth that stick straight out and make a special comb, called a tooth comb. They brush their coats with tooth combs to get rid of dirt and loose fur.

Ring-tailed lemurs are very neat animals. They will groom throughout the day, although most fur cleaning is done during quiet periods. Troop members often take turns grooming each other. Mothers will clean their infants' fur until the infants can groom themselves.

People and Ring-Tailed Lemurs

Many people enjoy watching and learning about ring-tailed lemurs. Some people have spent much of their lives studying these interesting animals. In some places, people even keep ring-tailed lemurs as pets.

The easiest way to get a close-up look at these busy animals is to visit the zoo. There are more than 1,000 ring-tailed lemurs in about 140 zoos all over the world. Lemurs that live in zoos usually have long, healthy lives. Some have lived up to 33 years! Why not plan a trip to your nearest zoo to see a beautiful ring-tailed lemur and its long, striped tail!

arboreal (ahr-BOR-ee-ul) Having to do with trees.

bark (BAHRK) The hard outside covering of trees.

communicate (kuh-MYOO-nih-kayt) To share facts or feelings.

endangered (in-DAYN-jerd) Describing an animal that has almost died out.

groom (GROOM) To clean the body and make it neat.

mammals (MA-mulz) Warm-blooded animals that have backbones and hair, breathe air, and feed milk to their young.

mate (MAYT) To join together to make babies.

scent glands (SENT GLANDZ) Body parts that make smells that animals use to mark their land.

social (SOH-shul) Living together in a group.

spines (SPYNZ) Hard, pointed parts.

weaned (WEEND) Changed a baby's food from a mother's milk to solid food.

Index

Web Sites

Due to the changing nature of Internet links, PowerKids Press has developed an online list of Web sites related to the subject of this book. This site is updated regularly. Please use this link to access the list:
www.powerkidslinks.com/scat/lemur/